Best Way to Finance a New Car

By Ade Asefeso MCIPS MBA

Second Edition

ISBN-13: 978-1499687637

ISBN-10: 149968763X

Publisher: AA Global Sourcing Ltd
Website: http://www.aaglobalsourcing.com

1

Table of Contents

Disclaimer

This publication is designed to provide competent and reliable information regarding the subject matter covered. However, it is sold with the understanding that the author and publisher are not engaged in rendering professional advice. The authors and publishers specifically disclaim any liability that is incurred from the use or application of contents of this book.

If you purchased this book without a cover you should be aware that this book may have been stolen property and reported as "unsold and destroyed" to the publisher. In this case neither the author nor the publisher has received any payment for this "stripped book."

Dedication

To my family and friends who seems to have been sent here to teach me something about who I am supposed to be. They have nurtured me, challenged me, and even opposed me.... But at every juncture has taught me!

This book is dedicated to my lovely boys, Thomas, Michael and Karl. Teaching them to manage their finance will give them the lives they deserve. They have taught me more about life, presence, and energy management than anything I have done in my life.

Chapter 1: Introduction

For many people, their cars are extensions of themselves and their personalities. Whether it's a classic Aston Martin convertible or a brand new BMW, the kind of car a person drives can tell a lot about that person in general. Never mind about the guy with the junked out pick-up truck!

There is really nothing else quite like driving down the road on a beautiful spring day with all the windows rolled down. The fresh air invigorates you and there is something that is just right with the world when you can relax behind the wheel of the car you call your own.

But what if you do not have a car? Walking down the road on a beautiful spring day just isn't the same. We lament the person who does not have transportation. You have to bum rides off of friends and family. You find yourself looking at your shoes in a whole new way. You know the local bus driver by name. Depending on where you live, having a car to drive is almost a necessity.

So you decide you really need to get a car, but you do not have enough money to buy one outright. You are going to need some kind of financing, but there is a problem. You either have no credit, you have a little credit, but not enough to convince someone to loan you money, or you have bad credit. Think it is a lost cause and you are doomed to walk everywhere forever?

Well, do not worry. There are things you can do to buy that car regardless of your credit history. There are many options that you have even if it does not seem that way. People all over the country are plagued with credit problems, so you are not alone! Many companies specialize in getting people back on the road in their very own cars. It is not easy, but it is possible.

I have done extensive research into the problems of credit-challenged people and how they can buy a car without having to sell of body parts or robbing a bank. The good news is that more and more lenders are financing auto loans for people with bad credit everyday.

No matter what your credit history, this book will help you learn what to do to establish credit, repair your credit, and get the car you're dreaming of.

Chapter 2: What the Loan Companies are looking For

Your credit history is a summary of all transactions you have made in the past that have involved anyone lending you money or billing you for services. This can include credit cards, utility bills, student loans, and much more.

There are three major credit bureaus who compile these lists and based on your history, you are given a number that represents your credit worthiness. You ideally want this number to be 680 or higher. If you make late payments, go into default on loans, or do not pay your bills at all, your credit rating will go down – sometimes dramatically.

These companies send reports to each of the three major credit reporting companies on transactions that they have undertaken with their customers. The credit reporting companies then put together the information onto your credit report.

In the US you are entitled to receive one free credit report per year thanks to federal legislation that went into effect a few years ago. All you need to do is go to www.freecreditreport.com and request a copy. Once you get your credit report, it is very important that you go over it with a fine tooth comb to make sure the information is accurate. You are entitled to make corrections if any of the data is wrong. Just contact the credit reporting agency and provide documentation that shows the wrong entry is incorrect and they are required to correct it.

When you go to apply for a car loan, the finance company will be looking for a few specific things on your application. First and foremost, they want to see documented monthly income. To get the lowest interest rate, it will need to be $1,600 or more in the US and similar in the UK.

They want people with established living and working situations. This means being at your present address for six months or more and being with same employer for six months or more.

They ideally would like for you to have a year of established credit with no black marks during that time frame. That means no late payments, no excessive credit card applications, and no previous loan defaults.

To get the lowest interest rates possible, your credit score should be 680 or higher. With a credit score of 600 to 680, you will pay a higher rate like 10 to 15 percent. If your credit score is below 600, it is very difficult to get approval, and below 550 it is nearly impossible – at least through traditional means.

For some people, paying a higher interest rate, this can be extremely detrimental to their monthly expenses. Not only will your car payments be higher each month, the interest you will pay is almost 6 times that of a loan with a lower interest rate.

With that information in mind, you can see how urgent it is for you to establish healthy credit, and maintain a healthy credit score, or you will spend your whole life wasting your meager earnings on interest, when it should be building your nest egg. This is why most people, even those ready to retire are broke. A lifetime of careless spending habits, paying only the minimum monthly payment, and paying full price for everything has left them with no nest egg.

So, if you do not have any credit at all, this is a great time to start establishing a credit history that you can be proud of.

Chapter 3: Getting Some Credit

If you have never had credit in your own name, it can be difficult to get a <u>car</u> loan or credit card. Having no credit history can be as much of a problem as having a bad credit history. Students, other young people, and newly divorced or widowed women who have always obtained credit jointly with their husbands often find themselves in this situation.

It seems like a vicious circle: you cannot get credit because you have never **had** credit, but you have never **had** credit because you cannot **get** credit. What is a person to do? You need to get some credit. Do not worry; it is not as difficult as it sounds.

The best way to establish a credit history is to apply for a small loan or line of credit from your local bank or a credit card from a local department store. Ask whether they report to a credit bureau. If they do not, having the card or loan won't help you establish credit.

To get a credit card without a cosigner, you must be at least 18 years old and have a source of steady income. Gas cards are relatively easy to get. Apply for one and use it to establish credit, but pay it off every month to show that you can pay your bills responsibly.

If you cannot get a small loan or gas or department credit card on your own, try to find someone to co-sign for you. Again, make payments regularly and on time.

You can increase your chances of getting the loan you are applying for by coming up with a large down payment. This generally means 20 percent of the price of the car.

So if you are looking at a car that costs £6,000, you should ideally be able to put £1,200 down. If you do not have the cash, consider borrowing from a family member or looking at a lower priced car.

When you put money down on your car, this decreases the amount of the loan you will need for the rest of the car and you increase the chances you will get the loan.

If you do not have a checking account in the US or Current account in the UK, open one. You have very little credibility with lenders if you do not have at least a checking account and preferably a savings account as well.

Just as importantly, be sure not to overdraw your bank account. Bouncing checks sends a signal to potential lenders that you cannot manage your daily finances and are therefore not a good credit risk.

Know what lenders and credit card issuers look for when issuing credit. There are other factors that affect credit approval besides just your payment history, such as how often you move and how often you change jobs. It also helps if you have had an apartment or utility in your own name. If you do not have a telephone number in your own name, you may find it more difficult to get credit.

If worse comes to worst, you may find it necessary to get a secured credit card. These cards require you to deposit money in an account to secure the loan or credit limit, and they often have fees and higher interest rates. If you default on your payments, the lender takes the money from your account.

After a few months of making payments on time on the secured credit card, you may be able to obtain a regular credit card. Remember to make sure the company reports to a credit bureau before applying for a secured card, or the card won't help you establish a credit history.

Before you apply for a credit card or <u>car</u> loan, get your ducks all lined up. Think like a lender. Applying to a number of credit cards in a short period of time can decrease your chances of getting approved. Lenders see this activity on your credit report and steer clear because they think you are getting in over your head, so pick and choose carefully and have a plan of action.

Being rejected for credit can also look bad. Apply only to cards whose requirements you are likely to meet. Read the small print and call the company to make sure your income and other factors qualify you for the card. Just because you get an offer in the mail does not mean you qualify.

With careful planning and a little knowledge of how lenders issue credit, you CAN establish a credit history fairly painlessly. There are many businesses waiting in line to take advantage of you by charging exorbitant fees or interest rates, so be careful out there.

Be sure to pay your utility payments like phone bills, utility bills, and rent on time. Every time you are late, it affects any credit you have in a negative way. Since you are just establishing your credit, you want to keep it as clean as possible so that you can benefit as much as possible.

It generally takes about six months to establish a credit history, so it is a good idea to get started on it BEFORE you want to buy a car. Your chances are slim to none at getting a car loan financed without some type of credit history, so start early and maintain it all costs to avoid problems in the future.

The same concepts should be applied when you have bad credit and want to repair it. Everyone makes mistakes and most people run on hard times occasionally. Even if you have had to declare bankruptcy, there is still hope for repairing your credit.

Chapter 4: Repairing Bad Credit

When you have bad credit, it can keep you from realizing your dreams. It is more difficult to buy a house, get a student loan, and get a car. When you can get credit from someone, the interest rate is usually exorbitant and you end up paying a considerable amount more than the purchase price of whatever you are buying.

The key to repairing your credit is to take an aggressive pro-active approach. It will take some time, but in the end, it will be well worth it.

The first step is to get a copy of your credit report. As I told you in a previous chapter, you are entitled to one free credit report per year in the US when you request one at www.freecreditreport.com. In the UK you can get free report at www.creditcheckinstantly.co.uk. Once you have the report, go over it and make a plan.

Begin by trying to resolve the outstanding debts that are showing on the report. The idea here is to make as much restitution you can toward settling the bills that have caused you to get bad credit in the first place. A horrible but old and closed bad credit item most often gets viewed better than an open current bad credit item.

How do you resolve these issues? Contact the creditors and ask about making a re-payment plan. If you have huge credit card debt, for example, often the companies will work with you to make a payment plan just so they can recover some of the bad debt.

If there is any way you can pay off the credit card entirely, that would be the best option. Ask if they are willing to settle for less than the entire amount due. They will be more likely to do this if you can offer them an amount of money that would be acceptable. In other words, if you owe £3,000 and can offer them £2,000 to discharge the debt, they are more likely to accept this than if you offered them £500.

After a certain period of time, some companies will "charge off" the debt owed to them. A charge off does not mean that a forgiveness of debt occurs, it only indicates the creditor has made an accounting notation that they do not believe that the debt will ever be repaid. A charge off represents a significant black mark on one's credit report.

Another viable option, although it is often thought of as extreme, is to file a Chapter 7 bankruptcy. In this context the bankruptcy paves the way to the first step of credit repair by putting an end to the old bad credit items. While bankruptcy adds it's own significantly terrible credit reporting item, bankruptcy by definition will be "resolved" when the case ends.

In terms of a credit report a bankruptcy is not a clean slate. A bankruptcy remains a nasty item on one's credit report for as long as ten years. On the positive side, however, the bankruptcy is a clear time or "line in the sand", from which the debtor can begin to rebuild. With open unresolved charge offs there is no such point in time where rebuilding can start. Open unresolved charge offs remaining glaring poor credit cavities on ones credit report.

A bankruptcy is certainly not a favorite resolution by the creditors but it shows that the debtors have recognized there is a problem and has taken some action. When you have open items or charge offs left on your credit report, it indicates that you were/are apathetic about the charges and do not care to try and make resolutions of the problems.

Once you have tried to make resolutions on the outstanding debt you have, the next step is to assess how much damage has been done and how you can go about reversing that damage. After you have paid as much debt as you can, you should get another copy of your credit report from one or all of the major credit reporting agencies. I will give you contact information at the end of the book for these companies.

You can only receive one free credit report per year, as I have said, so requesting additional copies will probably cost you a small fee, but we highly recommend this so you can better understand where you are after you have attempted to mend the past due balances.

It is very important to pay particular attention to any items that may be incorrectly reported. Many of those unfamiliar with credit reports share a mistaken belief that credit reports display a near perfect accuracy. In reality errors on a credit report occur with alarming frequency. Reporting agencies rarely verify or cross check information unless they have a specific reason to do so.

Inaccuracies on a credit report may take several forms including reporting of credit information on items which were never associated with the individual in question, items which may be related to an individual but are reported improperly or items which may be attributed to the individual but should no longer be reported on a credit report. Important personal items are often miss-reported as well including ones address, social security number and employment history.

If you discover inaccuracies on your credit report, responsibility lies with you to begin the corrections process. Letters must be written explaining exactly what the problem is and the remedy you feel is warranted.

Especially when dealing with inaccuracies, remember that each credit reporting agency maintains its own database of information. Therefore one agency might report an item properly while others report it improperly and vise versa. Furthermore, if a common inaccuracy exists with multiple reporting agencies the repair process must take place with each agency reporting the item inaccurately individually.

In many cases this means to remove an item that has made its way onto each bureaus agency report, you must write three sets of letters and follow the process through with all three different agencies in order to be sure an item comes off from the reports. Depending on how many incorrect items you have on your credit report, this could mean writing and sending out many letters, but you must be persistent. You deserve to be treated right!

Once notified of a problem an agency will contact the creditor or reporter of the item in question and seek a response regarding the accuracy of the item. Under the Federal Fair Credit Reporting Act if the agencies do not receive a reasonable proper response within 30 days they are obligated to follow your directives on proper treatment of the item.

Should a proper response be received the bureau may well request more information on why you believe your position be the correct one. Many people advocate dealing with only one item per correspondence.

Once you find you have completed this task follow up once again or check the report again. Just because a letter has been written and a creditor has not responded within a given time frame does not mean that the agency will remove the report without further follow up and an additional correspondence.

On the other hand keep in mind changes may take a month or more to appear on a report. While the process for proper credit reporting is in place, assuring accuracy of your own credit report rests with you.

Improving your credit score is one of the few areas of life where doing nothing can be tremendously productive. Once the items causing negative impact on the credit report have ended the simple passing of time does wonders for your credit score.

While the advantage of improving your score with the passing of time comes in the form of non-existent effort, the disadvantage comes in that time must take its own course. Even those with the best of credit cannot buy more time or speed the passing of time. Generally the date used to trigger the passing of time in this context starts with the date of the last activity of the account.

Your strongest tool for rebuilding your credit is staying current on your payments and not defaulting on any debt repayment plans. Even though we have said doing nothing helps tremendously in rebuilding your credit, repeating poor credit habits can make things much worse. Creditors can be somewhat understanding of a bad credit incident, if it is corrected.

This can be particularly true when the bad credit originated with problems outside of the debtors control such as emergency medical bills. Repeated bad credit behavior indicates a problem with deeper roots and looks to be a stronger indication that future credit worthiness looks shaky. If you want your credit to improve, be perfect with your new credit, as well as old credit where accounts remain open.

To accelerate the rebuilding process try to have at least three active credit lines open, and be perfect with them. Car loans or mortgages count if you still make payments, as well as old credit cards if they can still be used.

If you need to obtain new credit, store cards or gas cards can be easier to obtain than major credit cards. However, if those fall beyond reach, anyone can be accepted for secured credit cards. We touched on that subject earlier in the section regarding establishing credit.

Make sure when taking a new credit for rebuilding purposes that the creditor reports to the major credit agencies. Not all creditors submit information to the credit bureaus, and almost no debit card or check card issuers do, even ones with a MasterCard or Visa logo.

Use the credit you have obtained and make your payments on time. On time means never being 30 days late. At fifteen days you may pay a late fee, but late items must hit 30 days overdue before they will be reported.

Using credit does not mean abusing it; you need not run the card up to its limit. On the other hand, leaving the card in your wallet will not help rebuild your credit as much as positive usage. So, go ahead and use the credit card, just don't overspend and pay off the entire balance every billing period.

There are several companies out there who claim to be able to rebuild and repair your credit. There are also numerous debt reconsolidation companies offering their services. Are these viable solutions to your credit problems?

Chapter 5: Outside Companies and your Credit

First, let us say that there are definitely reputable companies out there who can help you with bad credit and overly huge debt hanging over your head. For some people, debt consolidation may be more attractive to you when you are in trouble with debt.

Basically, debt consolidation entails taking out one loan to pay off another. The advantages of doing this include securing a lower interest rate or simply for the convenience of making just one payment per month.

Debt consolidation companies can assist by discounting the amount of the loan. If you are in danger of major default or even bankruptcy, these companies will "buy out" the loan at a discount and then pass the savings on to you.

If you are in serious financial trouble and bankruptcy might be your only option to recover, be aware that consolidation can affect the ability of the debtor to discharge debts in bankruptcy, so the decision to consolidate must be weighed carefully.

Debt consolidation is often advisable in theory when you are paying credit card debt. Credit cards can carry a much larger interest rate than even an unsecured loan from a bank.

Keep in mind that consolidation loans are dangerous for impulsive people because all you are really doing is shifting all your debt from one place to another, effectively opening another channel of credit while freeing up your credit cards.

Some people then proceed to fill up their credit cards again making double the debt they started with, and paying up to 22% on their consolidation loan because they were not paying attention to the APR when they signed up. Some loan companies are real unscrupulous and make it look like they are eliminating your debt, or they hide the APR from you.

The best way to consolidate your debt is to use a debt reduction program, not a consolidation loan. There are plenty of reputable companies out there who can help with this.

Try the non profit American Consumer Credit Counseling for more info or Citizen Advice Bureau in the UK With their program, they do not lend you money, they work with your creditors to negotiate lower APR, and you combine all of your unsecured payments into one manageable payment.

You get a reduction in your interest rate and monthly payment, which pays off your balances much quicker than you ever could on your own, because interest is either eliminated or greatly reduced.

People with property such as a home or car may get a lower rate through a secured loan using their property as collateral. Then the total interest and the total cash flow paid towards the debt is lower allowing the debt to be paid off sooner. This will incur less interest.

In practice, many people are in credit card debt because they spend more than their income. If that habit continues, the consolidation will not benefit them much because they will simply increase their credit card balances again.

Because of the advantage that debt consolidation can offer a person that has high interest debt balances, some companies can take advantage of that benefit of refinancing to charge very high fees in the debt consolidation loan.

Sometimes these fees are near the state maximum for mortgage fees. Plus, some unscrupulous companies will knowingly wait until a client has backed themselves into a corner and must refinance in order to consolidate and pay off bills that they are behind on the payments. If they do not refinance, they run the risk of losing their house, so they are willing to pay almost any fee to complete the consolidation.

Another possible scenario is that the person does not have enough time to shop for another lender with lower and may not be fully aware of them. This is known as predatory. Many, if not most, debt consolidation transactions do not involve predatory lending, but it does happen.

So what about those companies that offer to repair your credit for a fee? Some of these companies will legitimately help to repair erroneous items on your report others fall into the category of con artists and crooks.

This evil group starts off with the out right thieves - companies, which offer the world, take your money and do nothing. Avoid these by checking references including organizations such as the Better Business Bureau when applicable. Question how long they have been in business and pay attention to what they are telling you.

If their claims sound too good to be true you may wish to be on the defensive. When possible attempt to verify answers they have given you with independent sources. Ask how much time credit repair takes. No one telling you credit repair happens instantly should be trusted.

Some organizations claim they will issue you a new social security number or create a completely new credit profile for you. Organizations of this type fall into one or two categories, those who are scam artists and liars and those who are operating illegally.

Even if an entity some how could create a new credit profile for you such an action would be completely improper under the law. Any organizations making claims of new social security numbers or new credit profiles should be avoided.

Some credit repairs organizations do follow the rules and understand the system. Even with those who are attacking items on a credit report using the proper procedures can sometimes go too far.

Either at the request of the debtor or the suggestion of the credit repair agency some companies will wage a war with the credit bureaus concerning legitimate items in the hopes that the creditor either ignores the correspondence or gives up on the paperwork required with the result that legitimate bad credit items end up removed.

Companies such as this should be avoided as well. This type of credit "repair" could constitute fraud and might very well be illegal. The last thing you want to do is getting caught up in some type of improper activity when you are trying to get back on your feet.

The thing about credit repair companies is that everything they do, you can do yourself. All they can offer you is a way to take the burden of contacting the companies with which you have bad debt off of you. You have to decide for yourself whether or not it is worth the fee you will have to pay. In most cases, it probably isn't.

In general, you should probably avoid credit repair companies although the decision should be yours entirely. If you are thinking of hiring one of these companies, be sure you do your research and do not get caught up in empty promises. There are no quick fixes in credit repair. It takes time and patience to correct your report, and more time for accurate negative items to be removed from your report.

When it comes to credit repair, you are the expert because you know your financial history the best, and can spot mistakes more easily. Instead of spending money to repair your credit, spend your money to pay down your debt. You will kill two birds with one stone as paying down your debt will improve your credit score, and it will save you money you would have spent on interest.

So, now that we have addressed the credit issue, what about that car you want to buy?

Chapter 6: Finding the Right Car

The obvious first step toward buying your dream <u>car</u> is to figure out what kind of car you need to be looking for. You do, however, need to be realistic. We all have that idea in our heads of our dream car, but it just may not be feasible to get that particular car.

You should keep in mind that you are not only trying to establish and/or repair your credit, but you want transportation as well. Think within the parameters that make sense for you. You need to be sure that you can not only make the payments, but also that you get a car that works for you.

It is important to know what you can afford before you go shopping. It is alright to dream because you never know what you will come across in your search. You may find someone who is willing to part with a car that you have always dreamed of at a bargain price.

Look everywhere for your car. You do not have to be confined only to car dealers. Scan the want ads and see what people are selling on their own. This could be the best way to find a great car since you do not have to deal with a pushy salesperson.

When you find a car you think you want to see, make the call, but keep the following checklist handy when asking questions about that car.

TELEPHONE INFORMATION SHEET
(QUESTIONS YOU SHOULD ASK WHEN CALLING ABOUT A VEHICLE.)

Date:

Owner s Name:

Make of Car:

Year:

Color:

Mileage:

Condition – Including any Possible Problems:

5 Speed Transmission:

Automatic Transmission:

Asking Price:

Monthly Payments, if any:

Number of Payments Remaining:

Full Pay-Off Amount:

Are Payments Current:

Address Where Car Is Located:

Owner's Phone Number:

Comments:

You may think that asking this many questions may be an invasion of privacy or a bit intrusive. Get rid of that thought. Anyone who is serious about selling their car will be happy to answer twice that many questions. Plus, they are more likely to take you seriously when you project a prepared image.

If you think you might be interested in a vehicle, ask to take a test drive. However, before you do, research the car you are going to be looking at. There are many ways to do this.

In the US Kelly Blue Book is known as the "bible" of a car's value. Simply log on to www.kbb.com and answer the questions they ask to gauge the approximate value of the car. One of the questions will be what condition is it in: Excellent, Good, Fair, or Poor.

Before you go drive the car, you will only have the owner's opinion of the car. Many people over-exaggerate the actual condition in hopes of making the car sound better than what it is. I suggest that you enter in "Fair" prior to driving the car to get an approximate value. If the car itself turns out to be an excellent, you can always re-evaluate the price that Kelly gives you and decide whether or not the car is worth the asking price.

There are plenty of car lots out there who offer financing to people with credit issues. They usually come with names like "EZ Credit Auto" or "Car Specialists". A bit of a disclaimer belongs here. Those names were completely made up by the author. Anyone who has that business name is purely a coincidence and no offense is meant!

At any rate, many of these car lots can be a great help to people with little, no, or bad credit. You need to be aware, however, of what you will be offered at these lots. Most of the time, the cars they have are high mileage and older models (at least 10 years old). They will probably be a bit over-priced for their condition, although that is not always the case.

What these companies do is offer on-the-spot financing through their business at a high interest rate as well as higher payments. The advantage to using them is that you will be re-establishing your credit or establishing credit for the first time. This can be a huge benefit.

Be aware, though, that you might be getting yourself into a situation that might be too much for you to handle. Before you sign on the dotted line, be sure that you will be able to make ALL of the payments and make them on time. If you do not, you will just be in a bad credit situation which will only cause more problems.

Finally, you can try the traditional route and go to a regular car dealer. The salespeople can often offer you some options when it comes to financing, and they will often go out of their way to do what they can to see you buy a car. The reason is obvious, they want a sale.

The financing people at new car dealerships know a lot of alternative financing routes that you can take advantage of. They will also, most likely, have a much better selection of cars for you to choose from thus increasing your chances of finding a great vehicle for your specific needs.

No matter where you go to find your car, be sure to stand firm and stay within your means. DO NOT let anyone talk you into buying a car that you either cannot afford or are not crazy about. There are a bazillion other cars you could fall in love with. Be willing to walk away from the car if the deal does not meet the criteria you laid out earlier. Your ability to negotiate a great deal will increase by leaps and bounds.

Perhaps most importantly, get the vehicle identification number (VIN) which is usually found on the driver's side dash through the windshield. When you have the VIN, you can find out a lot of information about your potential car.

Log on to www.carfax.com and enter in the VIN. Once you do, you will have a complete history on the car including all previous owners, whether or not it has been wrecked, and much more information. Knowing this can make a difference in whether or not you buy that particular car.

This author cannot stress this point enough. I personally had an experience where I went to purchase a car from a dealership. The salesperson told me it was a "program" car which can mean a variety of different things – it could be a dealer car, a rental car, or an executive car among other things.

The salesperson assured me that this particular car was a car used by executives from the car company to use and that once it hit a certain amount of miles, it was offered up for sale. She said that it was used in a large city about 60 miles to the west of where I lived.

I was not completely convinced that I wanted to buy the car because of the payment. They were a little higher than what I wanted, but the car had relatively low mileage, was in great shape and it seemed like a good deal. I took the car home overnight and decided to buy it before I went to bed. Had I known about the Carfax report, I would have never signed the papers.

As it turned out, the salesperson lied to me. My car was not driven by a car company executive west of my town. It was a rental car in a major city 300 miles <u>south</u> of my town – and it had been wrecked.

I would never have questioned this until I began having some major problems with the car just three months after buying it. The problems I was having were not consistent with a car that was that new, and the dealership was not willing to make good on all the problems I was having.

The moral of the story is to do your research. If you are not sure about a car purchase, DON'T DO IT. Trust your gut instinct. Look very carefully at what you are going to buy and make sure that what the seller is representing the car as is the complete truth.

This will save you a lot of headaches and insure you have a positive experience when buying a car.

You may also want to ask a mechanic to give the car a good "once over" to see if there are any obvious problems you should be concerned about. Have a mechanic in mind and take the car to them preferably on your test drive.

Many people – individual owners and dealerships alike – will try to play the "I have a lot of people interested in this car" trick hoping that you will rush into the buy. Don't fall for this. If someone else gets the car, then it wasn't meant for you. Another one will come along.

We recently had an individual owner try this with my son. When he test drove the car, there were some major front end concerns and the gentleman trying to sell the car was attempting to pressure my son with this type of ploy.

Luckily, my son was smart enough to back out of the deal even though it seemed like a good car. Someone else got the car, but we take a relieving breath knowing that we are not the ones who will have to get the front end fixed!

There are so many things you have to keep in mind when buying a car, but most of all, I have three major points that you should never forget:
1. Do not buy a car you cannot afford
2. Make sure it is worth the money
3. Do your research and know what you are getting into

If you keep these things in mind, you will be on your way to car ownership!
But what about the money?

Chapter 7: It's all about the Benjamins

Ideally when you buy a car, you want to pay cash to avoid having payment that you cannot afford. Unfortunately for many of us coming up with enough cash to buy a car simply isn't possible. When you have credit issues, this can be a huge problem to car ownership. But it does not have to be.

The obvious solution to this problem is to save up your pennies and buy a car once you <u>can</u> afford it. But what if you cannot wait for a few years to save up that money? There are still some solutions!

You should first and foremost try to apply for a car loan yourself. If you go to a car lot that does self-financing, they will ask you to apply for credit with them. You will have to fill out a credit application, but don't stress out about it. They specialize in getting people with less than perfect credit financing for cars.

The downside is that you will pay a high interest rate as I have talked about before. Plus, you are limited to just the cars that they have on their lot. The upside is that you will be on your way toward getting credit established or re-established.

You may also want to consider finding your own financing. There are plenty of places that you can go to that cater to people with little credit, no credit, and bad credit who are willing to loan you money to buy a car.

The good news is that buying a car is not a huge expenditure like buying a house is. More companies are willing to lend you money for transportation. But you will probably have to pay more in interest. The trade off is necessary when you have no credit or bad credit.

Your best bet is to apply online to a company that specializes in credit problem loans. Over the last 10 years the amount of money being loaned to people with poor credit has tripled.

Even with bad credit, you can probably still get approved for a car loan. Applying online will save time and money. There are companies on the internet that will offer you auto loan quotes from more than one lender in order to ensure that you get the most competitive quote you can qualify for.

If you are looking for an auto loan online, remember to use primarily vehicle loan companies that will help you compare quotes and offers from more than one lender. This will help you get the lowest interest rate and best terms possible. Also, make sure to fill out your application as accurately as possible in order for the lender to give you the most realistic offer they can.

Many online car loan companies have programs to finance people with bad credit history. Whether you have a recent bankruptcy, foreclosure or another adverse credit blemish, you may still be able to qualify for a car loan. Having poor credit nowadays will not keep you from getting financing. Even if you have no credit, you may still be able to get approved.

Do your homework with these companies and ask questions. They benefit by lending you money and you can benefit by being able to purchase a car! Be honest with them when communicating and you will end up in the best situation they can possibly offer you.

Poor credit auto loans make it possible for people with bad credit to buy a car. Poor credit auto loan lenders expect to be approached by people who have poor credit so they don't set strict requirements for their loans.

With a poor credit auto loan, people with bad credit can obtain a car without all the hassle of worrying about their credit or being repeatedly turned down. Despite some benefits, though, there are also disadvantages to getting a poor credit auto loan. Both should be considered before any driver tries for poor credit auto loans.

As a plus for poor credit auto loans, they are fairly easy to obtain. Poor credit auto loan lenders tend to require that you have steady employment and a decent debt-to-income ratio.

Although they will usually look at your credit, it is not a major factor in the loan approval process. It does, however, dictate your interest rate as I have already told you. The poor credit auto loan lender will look at your credit history to determine how great of a risk you are. The worse off your credit is, the higher your interest will most likely be for poor credit auto loans.

Consider trying your own bank for poor credit auto loans. Since they know you better than other lenders, they may be lenient with you.

We have a note here on the time frame of your loan. It is generally a good idea to only take out a loan for no more than 48 months (4 years). Most people choose the 60 month (5 year) option because their payments will be lower.

However, vehicle ownership entails more than just the car payment. You need to add in insurance, gas, repairs, etc. when considering what you can afford in a car. You do not want to spend the next 5 or 6 years paying off a car that will depreciate in value the moment you drive it. You run the risk of ending up in a situation where you will owe more than what the car is worth.

Another solution to car financing is to find a co-signer to apply for the loan with you. Most often, this would be a parent or spouse, but anyone can co-sign for you. Of course, you will want them to have good credit to improve your chances of securing the loan.

A co-signer will sign the credit application basically saying that they are willing to back you in the purchase of this car. They are agreeing that if, for some reason, you do not make the payments, they will be responsible for re-payment of the loan.

This is a big deal for your co-signer because they are putting their credit score on the line for you. It is important for you to realize that if you do not make your payments, you are not only jeopardizing your credit, but theirs as well. Plus, if you do not make the payments, the <u>car</u> will be repossessed and future liens could be put on their income.

When you ask someone to co-sign for you, be very conscientious about what you are asking them to do. Some people just are not willing to take the risk, so do not be offended if they say no.

Since their name will be on the loan, it will appear on their credit report as an additional item. This could affect their borrowing ability in the future since most lending companies look closely at debt-to-income ratio before they give out money. Carrying too much debt including your car loan could cause them to be turned down when applying for credit.

When you apply with a co-signer, your name and their name will be on the loan. This means the loan is really in the names of two parties at once, but it does benefit you by establishing credit in your name, as it is also in your name.

Having a co-signer is a risky and delicate matter for many people as it is a gamble for them to trust you completely to fulfill the loan commitment. However, if you are serious about establishing your credit or rebuilding your credit, there is no reason why it has to be such a risk.

One warning about co-sign loans is there are some real unscrupulous car dealers out there, who lie to you and say you are getting a co-sign loan. Then they trick the cosigner into signing the wrong line of the loan papers and the loan ends up in their name alone, instead of both of your names together. This is known as a Straw Purchase.

They pull this scam because they know you would never get approved, and they just want to sell the car, and it happens ALL the time. The law requires both people to be present and sign at the same time, and you need to make sure the correct names go on the correct lines of the application, identifying you as the borrower, and the co-signer as the co-signer.

There is one other option you may want to look at when it comes to buying a car. You can try and take over payments from an individual seller who is no longer able to afford their car.

A few years ago an industry emerged that served the needs of individuals who have had past credit problems, but can now afford monthly car payments. These companies help people with past credit problems. They will find vehicle owners who can no longer afford their monthly payments and match them up with people who can afford to make car payments but have trouble getting financing.

These owners would gladly allow someone to take over payments on their vehicle in order to save their credit, with no credit check. These companies charge the buyer between $1,500.00 and $3,000.00 for their services just to put these two parties together, without doing a credit check. However, you CAN do this on your own with a little know-how.

Start by looking in the local newspaper for newer model cars with a higher asking price – over $9,000 is a good starting point. Most people will not own a newer model car outright and be asking a higher price, so chances are good that they still have a lien on the car.

The easiest owner to work with is one who is considering letting his car go back to the lien holder for repossession. You can find these owners in your local newspaper or local car magazine.

Best results are obtained in aging these issues for two or three weeks before calling. The owners will always become more flexible the longer they try to sell their vehicles if you focus on ads proclaiming "Take over payments" or "Down and take over payments". These are individuals who realize that they are in a negative equity situation and cannot sell their vehicle outright.

Even though their ad might request a down payment, they will almost always waive it. Most lenders who recommend to the seller that he finds someone to take over his payments will still hold this individual liable for the payments if there is a default.

Many of these lenders will request an application to be submitted from the assignee. If the seller has been making his payments on time, the lien holder may want to keep him in this vehicle. They will want the buyer to have a stronger credit rating than the seller, before they will give their approval at all.

Traditionally, the companies mentioned earlier do not even contact or go through the lien holder. The seller still remains liable for the payments, whether or not an application is submitted. This arrangement allows the owner to monitor his own payments so he is actually more secure, as is the lien holder.

The companies contend that under the Uniform Commercial Code, Article 9. Section 311, the owner of a vehicle has the right to assign his property regardless of provisions in the original purchase contract by the lien holder (which might claim such a transaction to be in default).

The lender will always hold the original owner primarily liable for payments. Even though the payments are submitted by the buyer, the lender will still acknowledge the seller as the driver and owner of the vehicle. This is because the assignment agreement is between the assignee/buyer and assignor/owner, and not between the assignee/buyer and the lender.
When you have identified several cars that you have an interest in, you are ready to make the initial contact with the owner. Throughout this conversation your goal will be to find out if the owner is in a negative equity position (or upside down) on their vehicle. Best results are obtained if the owner is just asking for

what he owes on the car. Be sure to project a professional telephone personality.

You will typically have to make twenty or more phone calls to find a vehicle owner willing to assign his vehicle. One very important thing to remember, be persistent... keep calling. There are thousands of desperate people needing to get out of their vehicles in every area of the country. It is also a good idea to call the owner back a week or so after your first contact. The longer he sees that he cannot sell his vehicle, the more eager he will be to work with you.

The owner will normally want the car out of his name. His credit is riding on your making the payments. You will need to show him that he is secure and protected in dealing with you. When meeting face to face, it is extremely important that you present yourself in a professional manner. Treat this meeting as you would a job interview. This person is essentially giving his approval of you to assume his investment.

Once you have seen the car and feel that it is what you want, you are ready to make a proposal. Explain to the owner that you earn more than enough income to afford this car payment, but you cannot get financing from a bank because of some credit problems that you had in the past or because you do not have enough credit.

Tell the owner strengths about yourself that show your stability and credibility. That should include:

1. The length of time you have resided in your house or in the area.
2. The length of your current employment.
3. Your job description or job title.
4. Home ownership if applicable.
5. The reason for your credit problem.
6. If you paid back past creditors.
7. What your income level is with bonuses, future pay raises or possibly a job promotion.

Describe what makes you a good risk. Let the owner know that you are building his equity in this vehicle, until you pay it off. The more payments you make, the less will be owed on it.

Give him a copy of your credit report, personal references and a copy of your driver's license. Allow him to verify your employment and that you make your rent or mortgage payments on time.

Show them a copy of the suggested Assignment Agreement which we will give to you at the end of the book. You want to make them feel as comfortable as possible when dealing with you and having an agreement such as this could give them that security. This agreement would be a legal and binding contract with the two of you, so having it ready is a huge advantage for both of you.

Once you have satisfied all the owner's questions, and have subdued all fears, you need to get a commitment. If the owner will not commit and wants to think about it, find out when the due date is for the next payment. The closer he gets to the next payment, the more flexible he will become.

If the owner remains undecided, you may try offering him concessions. You could offer to make a whole payment or two payments in advance. He may request some kind of security deposit, which would be held for damages. At this point, be creative and willing to empathize with the owner's concerns.

There, of course, are some questions that the seller is likely to ask. Having the answers ready will reassure the seller.

1. What if you wreck the car?

    The insurance company will issue a check/cheque with both your name and the lien holder's name on it. This check will be applied towards repairing the vehicle.

2. What if you get a ticket while driving this car?

    Any points are charged to my individual driver's license, not to the car.

3. What if you hit someone?

    The Suggested Assignment Contract states that I am driving the vehicle, and am responsible for all liabilities. Your liability is limited because I will carry 100/300/50 liability coverage or whatever your Purchase Agreement with the lien holder requires, which will protect you. As the owner of this car, you are put in the same position as an independent leasing company or car rental agency. You own the car, but you are not driving it.

4. How do I know that you will make these payments?

You will receive a cashier's check/cheque or money order made out to the lien holder at least ten days before your payment due date. If I am late, you have the legal right to take the vehicle back. Believe me I do not want to lose it. The agreement basically states that I will make the remaining payments or pay it off early. As long as I do this, you are under contract to sign over the title to me. Nothing hidden, no surprises, it is fair and legally binding.

5. What about the license plates?

You are still the legal owner, just as leasing companies and rental agencies are. As such, the license plates on the <u>car</u> will have to be yours. However, I am the one who is primarily liable for what happens while it is in my possession.

6. What if you move and cannot be located?

I am giving you a list of personal references, my driver's license number and my social security number. Any repossession firm could track the car in a matter of hours. I can understand your concern, but let me assure you that I have no intention of going to jail for car theft.

As far as insurance is concerned, keep in mind that regulations differ widely from state to state. The simplest and most widely accepted structure for this arrangement is to list the owner as primary insured and you as additional insured. The loss payee will always be the lien holder.

The policy address can be that of either the buyer or seller. Insurance can remain on the existing owner's policy by just adding the buyer as an additional insured. The owner may prefer to set up a new policy so that the buyer's driving record will not affect the rates that he pays for his other vehicles.

Recommended liability limits should be $100,000/$300,000/$50,000: $100,000 maximum limit of liability per person, per accident; $300,000 maximum limit of liability for all persons per accident; $50,000 maximum liability limit for property damage, per accident. These higher liability limits normally will account for a minor increase in rates.

If the seller has a poor driving record, that would make your insurance premiums prohibitive; however, you do have some options. Some insurance companies will allow you to list the buyer as Primary Insured and the seller as Non-Driving additional insured.

They will treat the policy just like a normal lease. In the place of the leasing company, they will insert the name of the seller. The Loss Payee remains the bank or lien holder. Let the insurance company know that you have the Power of Attorney for this vehicle.

If this is the direction that is most economical for you, then you may want to find a creative, knowledgeable agent (this is not always easy). Many agents may reject your policy without fully understanding the relationship or legality of it.

It is generally recommended that you talk directly to the underwriters if the agent does not seem knowledgeable. If you do set up your policy in this manner, then you may want to contact the Department of Motor Vehicles in order to see if a lease tag can be issued in your name without changing the title.

When registering the vehicle, most states again have different policies regarding an agreement such as this. The most common is to register the vehicle in the seller's name in care of buyer's name and address.

You should keep Limited Power of Attorney with registration. In most states, limited power of attorney along with the assignment contract is sufficient to register a vehicle. Registration and license plates are to remain in seller's name, (normally leave the same license plate on the vehicle).

This may seem like an impossible arrangement and one that no one would agree to, but think again.

When a person has a large car payment and they are in danger of having the car repossessed, they want to avoid having such a large hit on their credit report.

Many people will explore whatever options they have to avoid repossession and the blemish it will leave on their credit. If you can show them that you are serious about owning your own <u>car</u> and that you can easily make the payments, this is a win-win situation for both of you!

Chapter 8: Timing is Everything

When you have little or poor credit, WHEN you try and buy a car can be a big issue. If you are thinking about purchasing a new <u>car</u> with bad credit, timing is important.

Sadly, millions of people are living with bad credit. Unfortunately, it takes time to improve or boost credit rating. Still, if you need to buy a new car, there are options. Before buying a car, carefully consider whether now is the right time.

If you are hoping to quickly improve your credit score, buying a car with bad credit is a wise move. Rebuilding or re-establishing credit is challenging. However, if you obtain an auto loan, and make regular payments, your credit will improve in as little as six months. Increasing your credit score opens the door for lower rates on future auto loans and credit account.

Because bad credit auto loans have higher interest rates, you must be in a position to afford higher monthly payments. If possible, finance a low amount. You may choose to buy an inexpensive car, or purchase the car with a sizeable down payment.

Chapter 9: Avoid Scams

When you are working so hard to get the car you want, you need to be sure you are not being taken advantage of by unscrupulous car dealers. Unfortunately, there are many people out there all too ready to sell you a lemon with high car payments.

There are many ways a dealer can try to scam you. Thanks to a great website, www.carbuyingtips.com, I can show you their top ten car buying scams and how to avoid those scams.

"The Financing Fell Through"

This is the oldest trick in the scam book, increasing in 2010. How it works is you buy a new car, the finance manager says you got a low APR, hands you the keys, and you drive home. Sometime later after you have been driving the car happy about your great interest rate, the dealer calls you saying "Sorry, you did not qualify for that low interest".

This is where "subject to financing" clauses on contracts bite you in the butt. Everyone thinks that you sign papers it is a done deal. The dealer knew exactly what you qualified for before you signed, unless you lied about your income. They knew your credit score when you applied.

There is a phrase on most sales contracts stating "subject to loan approval". This means that the deal is not final, even though you signed this contract. They will tell you that you must produce an additional

$1000 AND your payments would go up. They pull this scam on people with bad credit, because it is believable and they figure you will just pay up somehow so you can keep your car.

To avoid this scam, DO NOT FINANCE AT THE DEALER if you have bad credit. Line up your own financing and compare to dealer's financing. By using your own financing, you won't endure monthly payment scams, and the deal will be based on the selling price of the car, not monthly payments.

If they start negotiating the car by monthly payment, it is time to leave. If they keep trying to shift your APR up or down depending on whether you buy a warranty or VIN etching, it is time to leave. But if you do finance through a car dealer, leave a deposit on your credit card, and do not take delivery of the car until the loan has been approved in writing a few days later. Then you know the lender has approved your loan.

If this scam happens to you, you will have to decide whether or not you feel you got a good enough deal on the selling price of the car. If you got a good price on the car, your best solution is to preserve your deal and get your own instant financing online.

If the dealer refuses your online check, you should try to get out of that deal. File a complaint with the Better Business Bureau at BBB.com, and file a complaint through your state's Attorney General web site. They are all aware of Spot Delivery Scams.

"The Straw Purchase"

This type of scam has increased in recent years. Incidences of this typically increase when interest rates go up, and fewer people qualify for loans as lenders tighten their belts. Even though we touched on this scam earlier under the section on co-signers, it bears repeating because this type of scam can happen before you know it has.

A straw purchase traditionally refers to handgun sales. When one person buys a handgun for a person who is ineligible to own one, it is called a Straw Purchase, carrying stiff penalties. That is how the Columbine High School student shooters got their guns.

With car buying, the dealer tells you that with your horrible credit score, you cannot qualify for a <u>car</u> loan so you need to get a co-signer, plus they tell you that it will help build your credit again. The dealer knows your horrific credit score could not possible ever qualify for a loan, even with a co-signer.

So you find a co-signer who is duped by the dealer during the paperwork shuffle, and is tricked into signing as the primary borrower. Later, you find the dealer did not process a co-sign loan, the entire loan is in your co-signer's name!

Obviously, this does not help your credit, even though you are paying the monthly payments, because the loan is in someone else's name, and the car dealer lied to you. State laws are vague but some states like Texas have laws against Straw Purchases on cars.

You can avoid this scam by having both signers there at the same time when the papers are being presented. Both signatures should be on the same contract. NEVER sign separate contracts. There should be a separate line item for co-signer.

A notice to the cosigner is required by the Federal Trade Commission's Trade Regulation Rule on Credit Practices. The cosigner should ask for a copy of that before they sign it.

"We Forgot To Pay Off Your Trade-In"

You trade in your old car which you still owe money on, and the dealer is supposed to obtain a payoff figure and payoff the loan for you and add that payoff amount to your new car purchase. But something horrible happens. Some time later, you are shocked to hear the new car dealer did not pay off your old car loan as promised.

With this scam, dealers effectively pay you less for your trade than they promised or steal it altogether. When the bank calls, *YOU* are responsible for the loan, not the dealer. The car loan is still in your name, until the dealer pays it off. As far as the bank is concerned, they have a loan with YOU, not a dealer and it is in your name until paid off.

Then, your credit gets dinged with late payment alerts from your bank. If you try to sue the dealer, the judge will ask to see your contract with the dealer obligating them to pay off your old <u>car</u> loan. Of course there will be no contract and you are making twice the payments or ruining your credit.

To avoid the scam, it is recommended first that you not buy a new car when you still owe money on your current car. If you pay it off yourself first, you can get your title from the bank, and then trade it in or sell it privately. Then you can pay off your loan with sales proceeds.

When you trade in a used car on which you still owe money in order to buy a new car, make the dealer put in writing that he will pay off your car loan in 10 days, or there is no deal. Then the dealer is liable in court for that payoff. You do not want to end up in court without proof that the dealer was supposed to payoff your trade-in.

If the dealer refuses to put these promises in writing, it means they will probably pull this scam on you, and you need to leave immediately, taking your business to a more reputable dealer. It is the same with houses and cars, if you call for a payoff figure, you typically have 10 days to pay off that loan or interest will accrue. Most dealers are good, but a dealer who pulls this scam should know better.

"Lying To You About Your Credit Score"

This scam begins with the finance manager lies to you about your credit score, telling you it was really low, so you now have to pay a much higher car loan interest rate than you thought. This scam is pulled on people with good credit too, as it works well because most people do not know their own credit score.

Avoiding this scam is actually quite easy. No salesperson should know more about your credit history than you. You need to obtain a copy of your credit report and bring it with you to the dealership. If they try to pull this scam, pull out your credit score and put a stop to it.

Oh yes, and enjoy the look on the face of that finance guy when you pull out that credit report and show him you know he's trying to scam you. Then walk out of the dealership with a grand flair!

"Your Financing Check Bounced"

This scam is pulled on people who have taken the time to obtain their own financing and are able to go to the dealer with a check in hand from their financing company. The dealer sees your bank draft from a credit union, or online car finance sites. Not wanting to lose the extra gravy of selling you the car dealer's own financing, they refuse your bank draft, lying to you that "online lenders bounce checks."

They will say "their checks always bounce, so we do not take them". But by golly, the dealer is more than willing to provide you financing, at higher APR. Some financing companies are almost household names and many car buyers would immediately doubt the salesperson's lies. So the dealer may also tell you "well, they take too long to pay us".

Some salespeople stop at nothing. If your lender was bouncing checks, you did certainly hear about it. There is nothing wrong with dealer financing if they can beat your best APR. If not, use your online financing.

Unless you qualify for a manufacturer's 2.9% financing, online banks will beat the local banks used by dealers most of the time, and online lenders often beat credit union rates.

If a dealer spews out this scam and refuses your online financing, you the customer need to retain control and refuse to buy from that unethical and slanderous dealer. There are plenty of ethical dealers who eagerly accept online loans without the lies.

Tell the finance manager you are onto their scam, and that online lenders have been in business for years and fund loans without bouncing checks. Then get up to leave.

You should also file a complaint with your state Attorney General's office because this scam needs to be made illegal for dealers who force you into higher APR financing. If the state attorneys do not know this is going on, they cannot help consumers.

"Forced Warranty Scam"

This scam has been around for awhile and unfortunately, it is still in use. You are ready to sign papers when the finance manager says you MUST buy a $2000 extended warranty "because the bank requires it, or you won't get the loan".

OK, first let's take a look at this a little closer. The lender is worried about your ability to pay back a $25,000 car loan, so they want you to add another $2000 to the loan to qualify? Doesn't quite make sense, does it? Many people will fall for this scam.

Some dealers who quote monthly payments do not even tell you that you are buying a warranty. They tell you "it's included" to make it sound like it is free. The warranty is included, but you are paying for it. It is amazing how many people do not see it on the paperwork until they got home!

This scam often accompanies the Spot Delivery Scam. Some finance managers start playing games with the APR if you buy the extended warranty, some claim the APR goes up if you do not buy the warranty. Since when does the interest rate have anything to do with a warranty? They lie to you about this because they know that you know nothing about it. The only thing that determines the APR you will pay is your very own personal FICO credit score - nothing else whatsoever, not the cost of the car, and certainly not buying a warranty.

To try and counteract this scam, have them to put it in writing that the warranty "is required to be approved for your loan", so you can show it to your State Attorney, and the Better Business Bureau. Then watch how quick they back off.

This scam works on people with bad credit and they also "require" you to buy credit life insurance, or "your APR will go up". If they refuse to remove the extended warranty, remove yourself from that dealership immediately.

Many dealers sell you mechanical breakdown warranties, which are lame compared to some of the wear and tear warranties offered online. Also, dealers typically charge $500-$700 for gap Insurance. What is gap insurance?

Basically, gap insurance will pay the difference between what you owe on the loan and what the car is actually worth in the event that the car is stolen or destroyed. In general, gap insurance can be beneficial for you if you are unable to put 20 percent down on your car or if you roll the balance from your old car loan onto your new car loan.

You absolutely DO NOT have to purchase gap insurance from the dealer. It will be much higher than what you can find on your own. In fact, you can get gap insurance online for half the price that car dealers sell it for. So if the dealer tells you the bank requires gap insurance, tell them you will go get it yourself.

Another way to avoid the scam is to not FINANCE AT THE DEALER if you have bad credit. Finance your car online or at a credit union. Then they cannot force you to buy a warranty, you eliminate their excuse to force a warranty down your throat, and you have control over your car loan instead of them.

Credit unions and online lenders do not force a warranty or credit life on you, so why would a car dealer? Why does APR go up if you do not buy the dealer's warranty? Because of cash flow shell games. Remove their shells, and there are no more games!

"Dealer Prep or Excessive Fee" Scam

A better definition here might be "Excessive Charge", since this is not really a fraud, nor is it illegal. Most dealers do adequately disclose this fee on their paperwork. Many dealers even admit that it is a way for them to recover some of their "losses" when discounting the car off MSRP retail price.

However, this fee can be too excessive, and since it is printed permanently on their buyers form, what about the case when you pay full price on the car, and you have to pay $600 more in fees?

Salespeople try to convince you that a team of NASA experts performed a 3 day 15,000 point check of your car. Dealer prep "covers their cost" of removing plastic from the seats, vacuuming, adding fluids, and preparing it for sale. Total time: 2 hours max.

If a dealer charges a $600 dealer prep charge, you are paying them $300 an hour to make your car ready to go! Who in the world besides perhaps Bill Gates gets paid $300 and hour?

Do not fall for this. You see, the factory pays the dealer for pre-delivery service and it is already included in the MSRP. This is just a way for dealers to get extra money out of you.

Often, this fee is permanently printed on the buyer's order form to make you think it is mandatory, but many people make the dealer remove it by adding a credit on the next line. So if you see a $600 dealer prep on the form, have them add a $600 credit.

If they won't budge you need to decide how bad you want that car. You should have no problem walking out of a dealer over a $600 fee. Go to the next dealer on your list, and tell them "Here is the deal. Drop the dealer prep, and the deal is yours". Remember, Dealer Prep is not illegal, but it gives you zero intrinsic value. Either you agree with the fee, or you don't.

"We'll Pay Off Your Loan No Matter What You Owe"

These are common ads on the radio and newspaper all the time. They rely on your brain to trick you, as if the obligations of your current lease or loan just magically vanish. You cannot just dump a lease or loan, it is a contract. By breaking the contract, penalties are stiff, in the thousands.

When a dealer offers this to you, they *do* get you out of your current lease or loan, but payoff penalties must be paid to your leasing company to end the contract. The dealer is not doing any favors at all for you; they just want your trade in so they can give you far below market value for it, while selling you a new car at a high profit. Then they resell your trade in for a high price, while you are stuck paying off the debt load of 2 cars.

With this scam, if you are upside down on your car loan and you still owe $10,000 for it, the dealer pays off your loan, and then you owe that $10,000 to the dealer. This gets <u>financed</u> along with the $15,000 car you are buying; now you are financing 2 cars for $25,000! Your payments are spread out over 60 or 72 months so you do not notice what just happened.

The more months they add to the loan, the lower the payments so you do not notice. In fact, it is possible that the payments could be less than your current loan, so you think you are saving money when you just got shafted!

Their ad made you think that trading in a car relieves you of your obligation to that car. It does not! This gets many, many, many people deeper into financial trouble. You are actually taking on double your current debt, when you thought you were dropping one debt for another and buying a new car. They misled you.

Sure they did get you out of the lease or loan and into a new car, but you are not really out of it. They dipped you out of it and then dipped you right back into it under their umbrella of debt.

If you are in a lease or a loan now, it is best to stay in it until the end. If you are upside down on a loan, now is not the time to trade in the car. You need to wait until the car is worth more than what you still owe on it. Try selling it privately.

By mixing a trade-in with a new car purchase, you will lose the maximum amount of money possible. Don't ever think you walked away ahead on a trade in. No one ever has. No one ever will. If you really need to get out of your lease, shift your strategy from terminating a lease early to a strategy of transferring your lease to another buyer via an auto lease trade. You can find reputable companies online willing to do this.

"Previously Wrecked Car Being Sold As Is"

In this scam, the dealer tries to sell you a car that has previously been wrecked, only they tell you it is in great shape, they lie about the wreck, or in some cases, they were honestly unaware the car was wrecked. The car has the federally required Buyers Guide sticker with the words "As Is, No Warranty" on it, which means you are buying this used car and assuming all risks, and cannot return the car, because you agreed to all accept any damages that accompany your "As Is, No Warranty".

Even "Certified Used Cars" can be previous wrecks. Many people believe the dealer when they are told the car was never wrecked, and then they find out a few weeks later when they bring it in for service, or they run a CARFAX vehicle history report showing that it was wrecked.

When the scammed customers confront the dealer, they are reminded that they signed an "AS IS" paper, and have no recourse, because they cannot prove anything. The As Is paper is the best alibi the dealer has to fall back on. You however, have nothing to fall back on.

You really should never ever buy a used car from a dealer "AS IS" with no warranty. When you buy a used car from a private person you have no choice, it's "As Is". But from car dealers, try to get at least a 30 day warranty. If the car really is the cream puff they make it out to be, let them back that up with a 3 month warranty, otherwise they are just blowing smoke.

You should always run a Carfax report on any used car before you buy, and get it inspected by a mechanic. That is the best way to find out complete information about your car. Do this at www.carfax.com.

Always have a mechanic put the car on a lift BEFORE you buy. They can tell you in 30 seconds if the car was wrecked. Many people fail to perform these crucial 2 steps. If you do not do these steps, then DO NOT buy that car!

"Fake Vehicle Escrow Service"

This is actually not a car dealer scam, but it is a huge epidemic. It is a growing e-bay scam as well. Sometimes the scammers steal images from a car dealer and pose online as the car dealer. But mostly, these internet scams appear online as the seller of a used car. They place ads on Yahoo Motors, Auto Trader, Craig's List, eBay Auctions, eBay Motors. Every known vehicle and motorcycle classifieds site on the internet has been hit.

The scam begins with you buying a used car (or other product) online and you see a hot car with a selling price that is much lower than other listings for the same item. So you ask the seller a question. The seller replies with a "Dear Sir" form letter, rarely do they mention your name, it is all scripted. It usually has poor grammar and spelling too, and the seller claims to be in Europe and cannot keep the car.

Via email, they have you outside the eBay safe harbor, or whatever site you are using. He wants you to use a particular 3rd party escrow site, "he is used them many times already." Unknown to you, he just created that fake escrow site only a few days ago and he is lying. Plus, he is offering to pay shipping for the car! Do you know how much shipping is on a car across the U.S.? It is usually about $900. That is a big Red Flag.

They convince you to register on the "escrow" site, and you get payment instructions to Western Union or Money Gram the funds to the escrow company, then you never see your money again. No undo on the Western Union either, once your cash is wired, they can pick it up anywhere in the world in minutes.

There are many twists to this scam. They often trick you by telling you they are signed up for escrow with

Yahoo Motors, or eBay or Square Trade, none of which in reality do escrow or collect money for cars. You then receive official looking spoof phishing emails that appear to be from Yahoo, Square Trade, eBay, etc., with instructions on how to pay their "payment agents" via Western Union.

The scams have the same goal, to trick you into thinking you are sending thousands of dollars to a trusted escrow company. These fake escrow sites pop up at the rate of at least a dozen per day, with thousands of scam listings and auctions running all over the internet at any time. Now that you know what to look for, they are easy to spot.

NEVER EVER use cash wiring services such as Western Union, Money Gram, E-gold, etc, to pay for purchases online. They are all dangerously unsecured networks.

Do not use any escrow other than Escrow.com, recommended by eBay, and do not ever believe even the most realistic looking emails sent to you, as legit institutions would never send you sensitive payment instructions, you would login to get instructions. And never use the site recommended by the seller.

When you have no credit or bad credit, it is easy for people to take advantage of you, so be careful and trust your instincts. There are some guidelines for you to follow, too, when you buy a used car.

Chapter 10: Buying a Used Car

People with credit problems are better off buying a used car rather than buying a new car. While the reasons for this might be obvious, keep in mind that what you are trying to do is not only get yourself transportation but also establishing or re-building your credit.

A used car is going to be less expensive than a new one and you won't be stuck making huge car payments for a long period of time. Plus, by purchasing a used <u>car</u>, you can buy from a private party instead of having to go to a dealership where their prices are going to be higher.

The good news is that you can still obtain things like financing and warranties on used cars. Let's look at some general guidelines to follow when buying a used car.

The obvious first place to look for your car will be the newspaper classified ads or regional trader magazines. There are some places you can look online as well such as <u>www.cars.com</u> or <u>www.carsdirect.com</u>. Savvy consumers sell used cars online on cheaper and heavily traveled auto classified web sites.

Many services keep your ad online until your car sells, which newspapers do not do. This is an advantage of used car classified sites, many have 200,000 or more cars listed.

Once you have found a car you might want to buy, call and ask questions. We provided you earlier in the book with a checklist of things to ask the seller so keep this list handy and use it when talking with the buyer over the phone.

In addition to this checklist, also be sure to ask the following very important questions:

1. Why are you selling the car? Put them in a defensive position and they must answer quickly. If they hesitate, they have something to hide. Why do most people sell their car? Maybe they lost their job, or there is too many things wrong with it and they don't want to fix it, they did rather sell it to you. Maybe they bought a better new car and are selling it themselves.

2. How many miles are on it? The moment of truth for most sellers. This can really reduce the selling price if there is too much mileage. The standard is 12,000 miles per year. If they have more than that, the pricing sites shown above have charts that deduct off the market value of the car.

3. Do they have all the maintenance records, proof of tune ups, and oil change receipts? You just nailed them with 3 defensive questions in a row. They probably will not have this information, however, everyone SHOULD! This can be a powerful negotiating tool plus if you go to sell a car, it can bring a quick sale.

The seller might say "No one keeps that stuff". Your reply will be "I do and everyone I know does. Without it, I have no validation that you properly maintained the car."

4. Have them describe the condition of the interior, the seats, make sure the dash is not cracked, find out about the paint, tires, A/C compressor, ask if the A/C runs cool. Is there any other known issues or needed repairs that you should know about?

After you have asked all the appropriate questions and still think you are interested in the <u>car</u>, it is time to make an appointment with the seller to look at and test drive the car.

Make an appointment to see the car during the day. At night you cannot see all that is wrong with it. If you make an appointment with a seller, show up 15 minutes after the agreed time.

Once the agreed time has passed, the seller is now going through total hell, thinking you are not going to show. He is probably had a few no shows, so this might make him more anxious to sell the car. By time you show up, his confidence has been knocked down a notch. You are using psychological tactics and, legitimate methods of pricing a car.

Always show up with at least one other person, and make sure you have your license with you, most sellers won't allow anyone without a valid license to drive their car. It is harder for a seller to say no and challenge 2 or more people than just one person, so always show up with an aggressive companion.

If you visit a seller to test drive the car and they don't let you drive it, leave immediately. There is no reason to stay because you are not buying that car. <u>You should never, ever buy a car without driving it first.</u>

When you get to the location, check the driveway or garage floor for signs of fluid leaks. Rust colored stains indicate a leaking radiator. Black or Brown puddles and stains indicate an oil or transmission fluid leak, and purple puddles indicate transmission fluid leaks. The seller may tell you that his car does not have any leaks, but a driveway never lies. Make sure the seller sees you bending over to scrutinize the driveway and garage for signs of leaks.

You will also want to look for evidence of a previous wreck or rebuild. Check the tires and windows carefully for evidence of paint over spray. Sellers put a cheap paint job on the car and lie about it being in a wreck. The cheaper the paint job, the sloppier the body shop gets. They get over spray all over the place, and that is your singing telegram that the car was in a wreck or rebuilt.

Take the seller with you on the test drive and ask questions when noises pop up. Listen for noises, rattles, or grinding sounds. If you hear rattling in the quarter panels, the car may have been in a wreck.

If the car is a manual transmission, see if the shifting is smooth. Ask the seller if the clutch has been replaced. Clutches tend to fail after 4-5 years. This sets up the seller for a low ball offer. Most people are unaware that manual transmission vehicles have lower market values than automatic.

Check the heater and the air conditioning to be sure they work. Drive it in the daylight when the sun is hottest, to see how the air conditioning performs. Listen for grinding noises when the A/C kicks in. If you hear anything like this, the bearings in the compressor are worn.

If the car has a voltmeter, make sure the voltage stays at 13.6 volts when the A/C is on. You may want to bring a portable volt meter with you. Not everyone has one, but many people do. You can usually buy them for around $20.

Measure the voltage across the battery terminals with the engine running, and the meter set to DC Voltage. The voltage should be at least 13.6 Volts with the engine running, and no more than 14.8 volts. If it is not, there is a problem with the charging circuit, most likely the alternator, which is a costly component, usually about $150 rebuilt. If the battery is not at least 13.6V with the engine on, the 12V battery will not remain charged, and will die soon.

Drive with the radio on and off. Test the speakers to see if they are cracked. Make sure the CD player works if the car has one. Take the car on a highway, main streets, and side streets to see if the car loses alignment, or bears to the left or right.

See how well the _car_ brakes. Drive sharply around some corners, and your companion is writing everything down. Make sure all the seat belts work, that electric seats work, look for missing or burned out bulbs inside and out. If the car has retractable headlights, make sure they pop up and turn on. Make sure the brake lights, reverse lights and directional lights work. Ask the seller when the brake pads were last replaced.

Check under the hood to see how clean the engine is. Is the radiator fluid green? If not, it's been a while since the radiator was maintained and the fluid has turned brown. Is there any windshield fluid? If it's low, you should be getting bad vibes, a sign that you are dealing with a lazy owner, who could not spare a few seconds to add a few ounces of windshield fluid when he is about to sell.

Ask if he did his oil changes on time and when the last oil change was. Pull out the dipstick and check the oil level of the _car_ as well as the consistency of the oil. If it is sludgy looking and black, it needs to be changed or has not been changed in awhile. Good oil is a golden brown color and the consistency of syrup.

Check the transmission fluid; it should be purple if it is fresh and slightly brown if it is older. It should NOT be black. Check the air pressure in the tires and check for uneven wear on the tread. Ask the seller when the tires were replaced last.

Ask the seller to point out all known defects, problems, issues, etc. with the car. If there are any subsystems, alarms, or computer indicators that are not functioning, have them point it out to you.

Ask if there is an extended warranty with the vehicle, and if it is transferable to you. Verify this with the warranty company. Ask to bring the car to your mechanic to check it out. If they say no, you have to wonder what they are hiding.

Once you have talked the seller's ear off with all these questions, there are a couple of things you can do. You can start negotiating price or you can take your information home with you and make a decision later. In general, it is a good idea to check certain things out before you start negotiations.

First and foremost is to get a Carfax history report at www.carfax.com. All you need is the vehicle identification number (VIN) off the car itself. Car companies began assigning VIN numbers in 1981. It is a unique 17-digit code that identifies a lot of information about the car. The average Joe won't know how to decode the VIN number, and frankly, who really wants to? This is what Carfax will do for you – decode the VIN and tell the story of that particular car.

The VIN appears on all cars, in the dashboard on a metal strip. You can also find the VIN inside the driver side door on a factory sticker, the passenger door, the trunk, the hood, and sometimes the engine and other major parts have one, or it is engraved.

Car makers place VIN stickers on the major accident parts like doors, engines, and quarter panels, which are broken down from a car when it is stolen. If they show up on another car, something is wrong; the car was stolen, or junked and rebuilt. Check, doors and panels make sure all VINs match.

When you input the VIN into the Carfax website, you will be given all the information about that car including previous owners, whether or not the car has been wrecked, and much more. This can be especially helpful in determining whether or not the owner is being honest with you.

You will also want to find out what the fair market value is of the car by looking up its Kelley Blue Book value. Go to www.kbb.com and input the information about the car such as the year, the mileage, extras like A/C, CD player, etc. This site will tell you what you should expect to pay for your used car.

You may be able to do this before you even go to look at the car. See if the seller will give you the VIN over the phone so you can do your homework before you take the car for a spin. Then you will be fully prepared to begin negotiations.

It is important to note here that you should never rush into a car deal if you are not comfortable with doing so. Some sellers may try to pressure you by telling you that there are many other people interested in the car and you should jump quickly if you really want to own it. While that may very well be true, you should be completely sure that this is the car you want to commit to. If the car gets sold to someone else, there will always be another car out there, so do not be pressured.

In fact, it is YOU who needs to be tough with the seller. After all, you are going to be paying for the car, so you need to get the best deal you can. Despite what you have been told, you CAN negotiate at car dealers as well. Most dealers pay $3,000 to $4,000 less than market value for their cars, so they do have some room to work with. Remind them of this and watch them give you a great offer.

With a private buyer, negotiating is much easier. They know what their bottom line price is – the trick is getting them down to it from the asking price! We told you that you should bring someone along with you when you look at the car. They can be amazingly beneficial to you during negotiations!

Have your partner be negative, pointing out every little item that erodes away at the seller's asking price, and confidence. A great tactic with huge psychological impact is to rub your finger over every major scratch or dimple, and shake your head in disappointment. The car dealers use this all the time, so learn from the best. You do not have to say a word, the seller reads it right off your face, and you have set him up for the low ball offer. Have your partner write down all damage.

Ask for the maintenance records expecting that he will have nothing to show you. You should keep this in mind yourself. It is important to save every record, and oil change receipt in a notebook. Just add each new one to the end, and you have a nice history record. Now buyers of your car years later cannot say you did not take good care of your car.

Of course, you should ask if the car has been in a wreck, staring them right in the eyes waiting for their answer. If the answer is yes, inspect the area that was repaired, and point out every tiny little flaw in that repair.

It is not a good idea to just try and chisel down their price. Your offer will be based on sound research yielding the fairest price possible, ignoring the asking price altogether. Offer what the car is worth based on market values given by car pricing sites and your research.

They will all have varying values, so get an average figure, and print out from all the sites. Do not forget to subtract for over mileage, and add for options. Many used car pricing sites have three categories of condition of the car which they report the market value of. The condition will be listed as bad, fair, good, and each has its own dollar value listed, similar to the blue books in the stores.

Most sellers do not know how to price a car, so when you give your offer, it may be far less than the seller's "Hail Mary" price. They will get all insulted, and tell you you're crazy, that is way below their asking price. You must then educate the seller that his asking price was wrong to begin with.

That is when you show him the printouts from all the pricing sites. The seller may show you other cars in the newspaper and say "*See, they are asking the same amount*". Just tell the seller that very few sellers get their asking price when they sell a <u>car</u>, so those newspaper prices he is showing you are inflated.

It may be that the seller has no research and may be arrogant and indignant over your offer. They are unaware their asking price is off base. They get infuriated with your "low ball offer", and may refuse to deal with you. They could simply need the money; the car is taking up space in their driveway, or any number of reasons. His pride won't let him sell the car at your price.

He may say, "Why don't you buy one of those other cars if they are cheaper? If my car is not worth it, why do you want it at all?" It is their last ditch futile effort to justify their price. He is trying to divert you from the fact that he cannot justify his selling price. Any seller using this strategy has just told you he has no valid research on the value of the car.

A seller who knows the market value would say "Here are my printouts from the car pricing websites. My price is in line with accepted standards". Tell him "We like your car, but the research we have shows that it is not worth your asking price".

Point out the defects, lack of maintenance records, etc. Tell him the printouts specify a car in good condition. Point out scratches, dings, rust, carpet stains, cracked dash, and any justification to offer even less than the car pricing printouts. Keep hammering him for his research and justification until you are the clear victor of that debate.

Tell the seller "You will have your garage back, you will have this cash which I am sure you can use, no more no shows, no wife nagging you about getting the car sold, no more renewing your ads." Just because he did not get his asking price does not mean he lost. Your suggestion that he is a winner puts him at ease.

Then your buddy chimes in, heads for car, motioning to leave. Your buddy says "he is not going to lower the price, you are just wasting your time, and you should go back to the other seller who was flexible". Your buddy reminds you the "other car" had lower mileage. The seller is listening to this exchange and panics.

He knows you are on your way out the door and his sales tactics have failed him. You must always be prepared to walk. There will be other cars. If his car was so great, it would have been sold already. Make your ultimatum to the seller.

There is no way you will pay more for *any* car than fair market value. Right after you say this to the seller, turn to your buddy and ask him where the next stop is on your list.

Your buddy pulls other ads out of the folder, and reads off the info. At this point you can head toward your car to leave. Hopefully this will make the seller hop into action and accept your offer.

This is what gets you a good deal. Your strategy is to keep the seller on the defense. Whoever asks the questions is in control of the conversation. Continue firing difficult questions at the seller, but be polite. Let your printouts be the "bad guy", not you.

Do not say "You are crazy! I do not think your car is worth this". Instead tell the seller "the research I have here shows that your car is only worth this". Now your friendly relationship with the seller is still intact, and you are the messenger relaying information.

How can the seller argue with data from car sites who are experts at pricing cars? Skillful treatment of the seller gets your deal signed for you. You can let them know their deal is lousy without hurting their feelings.

Eventually, you will get to the point where one of you will say "Yes". That is the fun part because you are getting a car! Before you drive away from the seller's house, make sure you have the title, a signed copy of the bill of sale or a receipt, the maintenance records, and don't forget to ask if there is a special wheel lug key or you cannot change a flat tire, and a repair shop cannot replace your tires.

Make sure you have all sets of keys, owner's manuals, repair manuals, and spare parts that the seller may have, like extra lamps, headlights, wiper blades that they forgot about. Be sure the <u>car</u> has a spare tire and jack. Make sure all brake lights and other lamps work, and check the fuse box for blown fuses, replacing any as necessary. You do not want to get pulled over by the cops for no brake lights on your way home.

You may want to have another oil change done. Ask the seller for receipts for the battery or alternator. Many auto parts stores have lifetime warranties on alternators, or will prorate a failed battery ONLY if you have the original receipt, so be sure to hold onto these receipts and keep them in a safe place where you can always get your hands on them.

One last note, it is always a good idea to have your financing lined up BEFORE you even go to look at a car. Whether you go to a bank or apply online, you will have an easier time negotiating when you can say you are pre-approved or even better when you have the money on hand!

Handy Web Addresses
Here are some websites that you should refer to when trying to buy a car with credit problems. Many have already been mentioned throughout this book, but all are valuable as you search for a car.
Carfax for vehicle history: www.carfax.com
Credit Reporting Agencies: www.equifax.com; www.experian.com; www.transunion.com
Online financing: www.autocreditfinders.com; www.eloan.com; www.capitaloneautofinance.com
Credit repair companies: www.consumerdebtdotcom.com; www.idebtassistance.net
Your free credit report: www.freecreditreport.com
Kelley Blue Book for a car's value: www.kbb.com

Chapter 11: Conclusion

Car ownership might seem out of reach for you if you have no credit or bad credit, but it does not have to be that way. There are so many options out there to not only allow you to buy a car of your own, but also to help you establish or re-build your credit.

All you need is some know-how and diligence. Stay on top of your credit report. Make sure it is accurate and up-to-date. If you have any outstanding debts that show up on there, take care of them as soon as you can.

If you have no credit, start slow and build it by taking out a gas or department store credit. Charge a few small things and pay off the balance off each month faithfully.

Get online and apply for loans through reputable lenders like Capital One and E-Loan. Then start shopping.

Take the tips in this book and be prepared when beginning this journey. It will all be worth it in the end as you become a happy car owner!

Suggested "Assignment Agreement"

This agreement is made and entered into the date indicated below by and between (assignee) and (assignor). Whereas the assignor holds legal title or interest to the vehicle described below and has same financed with (lender) having agreed to pay lender (monthly) for another months (note payments) with a residual amount of (if a lease). Whereas, the assignor is desirous of assigning or selling the vehicle and assignee is desirous of accepting assignment and/or buying the vehicle.

In consideration of the mutual covenants hereinafter made and for other good and valuable consideration the sufficiency and receipt of which is hereby acknowledged, the parties agree as follows:

1. Assignor agrees to assign the vehicle to assignee/buyer for the term of the assignor's note payments due his lender, and hereby authorizes assignee/buyer to drive same, but only for so long as assignee/buyer is current in the assignment payments set out below in paragraph two (2). The vehicle cannot be taken out of the state without written approval from the assignor. 2. Assignee/buyer agrees to pay as assignment payments for such vehicle, the monthly amount of assignor's note payments to Lender, and to pay same by cashier's check or money order made payable to lender and to mail such payment to assignor at least ten (10) days before the day of each month beginning on the 199 . Any late payments shall be in default of the agreement.

3. Assignee/buyer agrees to take out and maintain insurance on the vehicle satisfactory to assignor's lender and to name assignor as primary insured, assignee as additional insured and lender as loss payee. Assignee/buyer further agrees and does hereby indemnify

and hold assignor harmless from any damage or liability arising out of assignee/buyer's use of assigned vehicle.

4. Assignee/buyer understands and agrees that should he/she fail to timely pay any of the assignment payments called for above, or allow the aforesaid insurance to lapse, or should assignor's lender declare a default under its note or loan agreement, or deem such loan repayment or the collateral to be insecure, this Assignment/Purchase agreement shall terminate at once. Assignee/buyer shall no longer be deemed to be an authorized driver of the vehicle, and assignee/ buyer agrees to return the vehicle to the assignor or his agent immediately. Failure to do so shall result in the immediate repossession of the vehicle by assignor, its agent or the lender or its agent.

5. Assignee/buyer shall have the option to purchase the vehicle upon (a) its full and timely compliance with this agreement and (b) the payment of all note payments to lender. Thereupon, assignor will deliver to assignee/buyer the vehicle's certificate of title. Default under this assignment by assignee/buyer, or other authorized termination of this agreement, shall forfeit any option to purchase the vehicle that assignee/buyer may otherwise have had. Upon full compliance and satisfaction of the lien, assignor will have 30 days to deliver title to assignee.

6. Normally, legal title to the vehicle shall at all times prior to assignee/buyer's proper exercise of his/her purchase option described above, remain in assignor's name and possession if applicable.

7. During the term of this agreement, assignee/buyer agrees to maintain the vehicle in good repair and full operation condition. Any failure to do so shall be grounds for termination of this assignment/purchase agreement and assignee/buyer shall be personally liable to owner for the cost and expense of any repair deferred maintenance, other than for normal use and wear and tear.

8. Upon a 48 hour notice to the assignee/buyer, assignor has the right to inspect the vehicle at a location of his choice, no more than once a month.

9. Any additional or special provisions applying only to this agreement are written as follows:

10. This constitutes entire contract. This assignment agreement including any addendum's or exhibits hereto which are by this reference made a part hereof, contains the entire agreement relating to the assignment of the vehicle and shall bind and insure to the benefit of all respective heirs, personal representative, successors and assigns of the parties hereto except as herein above expressly limited. Any oral representation or modifications of this assignment agreement shall be of no force and effect, excepting modification in signed by the party to be charged. No delay or forbearance of assignor in the exercise of any remedy or right will constitute a waiver thereof and the failure to exercise or a partial exercise of a remedy or right shall not preclude a subsequent or the further exercise of the same or any other right or remedy by assignor. Assignor shall have no liability for any delay in delivery of the vehicle for any reason beyond the control of assignor.

In witness whereof, the parties have executed this agreement as of the _____ day of _____ 199_____, at

_____

_____

_____ Assignee/Buyer
Signature Assignor/Seller Signature

_____

_____ Print Name and Address
Print Name and Address

ASSIGNEE'S RESPONSIBILITIES

1. Make payments to assignor, by money order, cash or bank draft made out to lien holder/lender and forward to

assignor 10 days before due date. (NOTE: Put account number on money order or bank draft. Assignor will promptly forward this to lien holder in order to maintain his credit status.)

2. Provide copy of insurance, naming assignor as primary insured, assignee as additional insured and lien holder as loss payee.

3. Notify assignor of any change of address.

4. Provide assignor with credit application (included in this information package) and at least eight (8) personal references.

5. Provide assignor with original assignment agreement.

6. Receive all manuals, warranties and other information pertaining to the vehicle. Keep warranty in the name of assignor.

7. It will be the assignee's responsibility to pay for and keep current the collision and liability insurance, property tax, inspections, permits, and other taxes or fees pertaining to the vehicle. 8. Maintain the vehicle in excellent working condition as described in the owner's manual.

Power of Attorney

KNOW ALL MEN BY THESE PRESENTS. That the undersigned of the County of State of being the Registered Owner of the above ,described motor vehicle, does hereby make, constitute and appoint of County, State of true and lawful attorney in fact to sign in the name, place and stead of the undersigned, any Certificate of Ownership issued by the Department of Motor Vehicles of the State, covering the motor vehicle described above in whatever manner necessary to transfer any registration of said motor vehicle. Granting and giving unto said attorney in fact full authority and power to do and perform any and all other acts necessary or incident to the execution of the powers herein expressly granted with power to do and perform acts authorized hereby, as fully to all intents and purposes as the grantor might, or could do if personally present, with full power of substitution.

IN TESTIMONY WHEREOF. the undersigned has hereunto set _____

hand_____ this _____ day of

_____,19____ .

(PLACE NOTARY SEAL HERE)

X _____ Subscribed and sworn to before me X

_____ this

_____day of

_____19_____ .

Witness:

Address:

Notary Public in and for the County of
_____ State of _____

UNIFORM COMMERCIAL CODE Article 9
Section 311. Alienability of Debtor's Rights: Judicial
Process The debtor's rights in collateral may be
voluntarily or involuntarily transferred (by way of sale,
creation of a security interest, attachment, levy,
garnishment or other Judicial process)
notwithstanding a provision in the security agreement
prohibiting any transfer or making the transfer
constitute a default.

www.ingramcontent.com/pod-product-compliance
Lightning Source LLC
Chambersburg PA
CBHW051734170526
45167CB00002B/937